YOU CHOOSE

CAN YOU SURVIVE A DEADLY EARTHQUAKE?

An Interactive Survival Adventure

by Thomas Kingsley Troupe

CAPSTONE PRESS
a capstone imprint

Published by Capstone Press, an imprint of Capstone
1710 Roe Crest Drive, North Mankato, Minnesota 56003
capstonepub.com

Library of Congress Cataloging-in-Publication Data is available on the Library of Congress website.
ISBN: 9798875240768 (hardcover)
ISBN: 9798875240737 (paperback)
ISBN: 9798875240744 (ebook PDF)

Summary: You Choose lets YOU control the story! Readers choose their own paths while encountering earthquakes in three different scenarios. The outcomes are different as decisions are made throughout the book.

Editorial Credits
Editor: Carrie Sheely; Designer: Heidi Thompson; Media Researcher: Rebekah Hubstenberger; Production Specialist: Tori Abraham

Image Credits
Dreamstime: © Eric Broder Van Dyke, 46; Getty Images: Design Pics, 68, Feifei Cui-Paoluzzo, 102, iStock/adlaphotography, 71, iStock/fikretozk, 50, Morten Falch Sortland, 23, shaunl, 43, Spencer Grant, 62, Visoot Uthairam, 33; Shutterstock: Anton Starikov, 107, BronisArt_2023, 38, Denis Radermecker, 96, FXQuadro, 65, isoga, cover, Jack N. Mohr, 14, Jo Panuwat D, 75, Magnus Binnerstam, 91, Mattanin Nonchang, 26, My Good Images, 83, Peter Hermes Furian, 101, Simone Migliaro, 35, Stefano Tammaro, 18, Wiparat P (texture background), back cover and throughout

Printed and bound in China. 006461

TABLE OF CONTENTS

ABOUT YOUR ADVENTURE

YOU are going about your daily life when an earthquake hits. With everything around you thrown into chaos, what will you do? Danger threatens at every step—shaky ground, collapsing buildings, falling debris, and sinkholes. It will take smart choices to survive the quake. YOU CHOOSE what path to take. Will you stay steady and survive or stumble as the earth rumbles?

Chapter One sets the scene. Then you choose which path to read. Follow the directions at the bottom of the page. Your decisions will change your outcome. After you finish one path, go back and read the others for new perspectives and different adventures.

Turn the page to begin your adventure.

CHAPTER 1

MORNING RUMBLINGS

This morning started like any other. You woke up and got ready for the day. A busy life means sometimes you don't notice the little things. Or you might quickly dismiss them. You hear a rumble in the kitchen briefly, but you don't think much of it. It's likely a large truck passing by outside or noisy neighbors.

Or someone is playing bassy music, you think.

You head out, ready for the day's adventures. The weather seems nice, and there are only a few clouds. Good! A bright, sunny day always makes things easier for you and everyone else.

Turn the page.

As you take a sip of your morning beverage, the ground shakes a little. It makes you spill some on your chin and clothes. You quickly wipe it away and look around. There isn't a big monster vehicle coming down the road. You don't hear any music, either.

Others out and about have stopped to look around too. It's not just you. You've been here long enough to know it might be the preview to something bigger. Is there an earthquake coming? The past has had its share of "false alarms," but today, something seems different. This could be the real deal!

To work as an actor on a major motion picture in Los Angeles, California, turn to page 11.

To report to your shift as a firefighter/emergency medical technician in Hawaii, turn to page 45.

To go snowboarding in Japan, turn to page 73.

WHAT ARE EARTHQUAKES?

Earthquakes are natural disasters that occur when the ground shakes violently. These tremors occur when large pieces of Earth's crust called tectonic plates move suddenly. Tectonic plates are like puzzle pieces that are always slowly moving. But sometimes, two plate edges get stuck while the rest of the plates keep moving. Friction and pressure build where they are stuck. Finally, the edges unstick, and the plate moves suddenly. Energy is released. The waves of energy travel through Earth's crust, causing the shaking sensation people feel.

There is no way to predict when an earthquake will hit. There can be many small tremors before a big earthquake. Places where tectonic plates meet and slide are called faults and have earthquakes most often. About eighty percent of large earthquakes occur around the edges of the Pacific Ocean, an area known as the Ring of Fire. This includes California, Alaska, and Japan.

CHAPTER 2

SET FOR DISASTER

No one could believe you were moving to California to become a movie star. For the first year or two, you worried you'd made a mistake. It was really hard to get work on films and TV shows. You were a featured extra, or a background person, on a few movies no one saw.

But today, that changes.

A friend of yours told a producer about you. You got an audition and landed the part of Chris in the new disaster movie *Mulholland Mudslide*. The film takes place in the Hollywood Hills, and it's your first day on set.

Turn the page.

As you drive to the location, you feel a little nervous. This could be your big break, and you hope you don't blow it. At the stoplight, you glance up at the hills. You see *HOLL*, a few of the big white letters on the Hollywood sign. You calm down. You've practiced your lines and know your character. You're a good actor.

You park in a lot designated for cast and crew. A shuttle bus takes you and others up a steep hill to the set. Marco, a production assistant, explains what the day's shooting will be like.

"It's going to be hectic and loud today, people," he warns.

"Today's the big mudslide, right?" a guy with a tool belt slung over his shoulder asks.

"Correct, Davis," Marco says. "And we need your team at the tank right away."

You turn to Davis as he gives Marco a thumbs-up.

“A tank?” you ask. “Are we making a war movie now?”

Davis laughs. “It’s a water tank,” he explains. “My team is in charge of releasing the water that’ll make the mudslide.”

You get to the set and learn you’re not needed for about twenty minutes while they finish setting up the shot. You’ve got some time to kill.

To check out your trailer and go over your lines, turn to page 14.

To walk around the set and watch the visual effect crews work, turn to page 17.

You've never had a trailer before, so you're curious. You walk toward the cluster of trailers.

You notice only three trailers on set. One for Magda Raines and one for Wes Calvin, the stars of the movie. The third trailer has your name and one other on it: Esha Shah.

"And we're sharing a trailer," you say, only mildly disappointed.

You knock on the door and almost instantly it opens. Your costar pops out, all smiles.

"So, you're playing Chris!" Esha shouts. "Come in! Let's run through our scene together!"

She grabs your arm before you can introduce yourself. She's got her script in her hand. You look around and see her stuff is everywhere already.

"Okay," you say, "Where do you want to start?" As you open your script, you feel the trailer vibrate and shake.

"Whoa!" Esha shouts. Then she laughs.

The trembling stops after a few seconds.

"What was that?" you ask, a little worried.

"Probably the effects crew setting up the big shot," Esha says, waving it off.

Turn the page.

You've lived in California long enough to know earthquakes happen. There was a tremor earlier this morning. Smaller ones happen from time to time. Is this one the real deal? Or is it truly something the crew is working on? It is a disaster movie after all. You hate to be jumpy, especially on your first big movie.

To get out of the trailer to see what's going on, turn to page 20.

To stay in the trailer and work on your lines, turn to page 24.

You've been on movie shoots before as an extra. There's a lot of sitting around waiting for assistant directors to call on you. This might be your chance to see what happens behind the scenes.

People are walking everywhere talking into walkie-talkies. A golf cart whizzes past you, missing you by inches. Perched on a network of scaffolds is the tank. It's a giant circular vat with a large spout at the bottom.

Davis is up on the scaffolding, examining the device.

"Looks good," he says into his radio.

To your left, is the fake house built into the hill. It almost looks like an expensive real house. It's amazing to think it will get destroyed just for one shot in a movie.

The director, Pierre Vanderman, is a veteran filmmaker. In interviews, he talks about how much he dislikes computer visual effects.

Turn the page.

Buildings made for a film set

"Too fake," he's said. "I'm sticking with practical effects!"

Which means, he's not relying on computer graphics. His crews will build it and destroy it, capturing it on lots of cameras. Since there's only one house, the shot needs to be perfect the first time.

As you wander closer to the house, the ground shakes violently. People shout. At first, you think it's an effect, but everyone looks stunned.

"Earthquake!" someone yells.

Everything is shaking. Boulders are tumbling down toward the set. One of the trailers falls over and slides down the hill. From inside the house, someone is screaming. Maybe someone needs help.

Then you see people stumbling toward the shuttle bus. Are they hoping to escape or use it for shelter? Maybe you should join them.

To get on the bus, turn to page 26.

To run into the house set to see if you can help, turn to page 29.

“We need to get out of here,” you shout at Esha. You know the trailers aren’t completely solid, not like a house, and even houses collapse.

“It’s nothing,” Esha says with a nervous laugh. “It’ll pass.”

“I don’t think so,” you say, finding it hard to stand on your feet. Esha teeters too. Her expression changes quickly.

Cupboards pop open, dumping dishes and plates to the ground. The large lighted mirror cracks. Shards of glass tinkle to the floor below.

“Maybe you’re right!” she cries.

You push the door open and stumble out. Everything is shaking so violently that it looks blurry. Esha is right behind you. The movie set is completely chaotic. Crew members are falling down. Expensive lights are tipping over. Sparks are flying from broken equipment. Stars Magda Raines and Wes Calvin manage to duck into a limousine. A large metal stand tips over and crashes across the hood.

“We need to find somewhere safe,” you shout. Everywhere you look, there are potential hazards. The lights and riggings are everywhere. The tank full of water is held up by metal scaffolding. You can hear it creak.

Is that thing going to fall? you wonder.

To your left, is the house set the production crew built. It’s not a real house, but it might be safe. Esha is pulling you toward it. You’re wondering if going inside is a good idea.

To find a spot out in the open and away from hazards, turn to page 22.

To take shelter in the fake house until the earthquake stops, turn to page 31.

"There's no way that fake house is safe," you tell Esha. "It probably took them a week to build it. This earthquake will knock it flat!"

Esha looks panicked. She shrieks whenever anything falls and anyone rushes past her.

"What do we do?" she screams.

"We need to get somewhere out in the open," you shout.

"But we're on a hill!"

She's right. It's hard to find somewhere free of hazards up in the hills. You glance around and see a real house farther down the road. There are big glass windows facing the valley.

Near the cast trailers, there is a big, metal shipping container. You're guessing it was used to transport the production's gear for this shooting location. The doors are open and swinging from the constant vibration.

“Two choices,” you shout. “We hide in that container and hope for the best . . .”

“Or?” Esha cries, obviously not loving option number one.

“Or see if we can get in that house down the road,” you reply, pointing.

To hide out in the shipping container, turn to page 38.

To go to the real house and seek shelter, turn to page 41.

You are on a set for a disaster movie. Chances are the shaking is probably heavy equipment moving some set pieces around.

"Okay, scene 52," Esha says.

You flip to the part in the script and look at your highlighted lines. You've already got the dialogue memorized but practicing it with your scene partner is never a bad idea.

"It's just a little rain," Esha says, reading her lines. "I'm sure we'll be just fine."

You glance over at the small kitchen. The constant shaking makes her bottle of water ripple nonstop. Outside, people are shouting.

"Pssst," Esha hisses. "It's your line."

The trailer lurches suddenly. Before you can react, it's flipped onto its side, throwing you and Esha against the wall.

"We need to get out of here," you shout. You crawl for the door, but it's no use. It's blocked by the ground.

Then there's a loud crash followed by the rushing of liquid. *It's the water tank for the mudslide,* you think. Water seeps through the broken windows at your feet.

Something heavy hits the side of the trailer, and the next thing you know, you're sliding. The trailer flips and crumples as it rolls down the hill.

You wake up in a hospital hours later with a broken leg and collarbone. Rescuers pulled you from the wrecked trailer battered but alive. Esha wasn't so lucky.

THE END

To follow another path, turn to page 13.
To learn more about earthquakes,
turn to page 99.

You want to be in movies, not a real-life disaster. Joining the others on the bus seems like the best choice.

The ground vibrates, making it difficult to run. Tents collapse with people beneath them. A camera tips over on its tripod, smashing on the hard ground. Panicked people fall into one another in terror.

You reach the bus just as the door hisses closed.

“Don’t leave without me!” you cry, pounding on the glass. The driver opens the door.

“Get in!” he shouts, waving you aboard. You climb the steps quickly.

The bus lurches forward, throwing you back down the aisle. You grab a seat next to a familiar face. It’s Magda Raines, one of the stars. She watches the set fall apart from her window.

You glance past her. The large tank of water shifts and creaks on the scaffolding pipes. Water sloshes over the side.

“Hang on!” the driver yells. You instinctively grab the seat in front of you.

Someone shouts, and you turn to look. An expensive sports car tumbles downhill toward the bus. It flips and turns, a wrecking ball of crunching metal.

“No!” Magda cries.

Turn the page.

The car slams into the side of the bus. It knocks the bus off course, and the driver loses control. The guardrail doesn't help. The bus plummets off the hill and crashes far below. There are no survivors.

THE END

To follow another path, turn to page 13.
To learn more about earthquakes, turn to page 99.

No one is trying to get to the house. If someone needs help in the fake structure, you might be their only chance. You dodge fallen equipment, knock into others scampering for safety, and reach the house.

The doorknob vibrates in your hand, reminding you of the earthquake's awesome power. You remember most tremors only last a few seconds to a few minutes. Somehow, this one seems longer.

You open the door and step onto the quivering floorboards. Furniture is scattered everywhere. Chairs are overturned. A glass cabinet is smashed on the ground.

"Hello?" you shout, holding the doorframe for support.

"Hey," a familiar voice cries from a back room. "Over here!"

You move as best you can among the obstacles and heaving floor. You hear a wooden snapping sound, making you wonder how secure the house is.

Turn the page.

You finally make it to the kitchen door. The floor is severely slanted.

Did the earthquake do that? you wonder.

In front of you is a refrigerator lying face down. A pair of legs poke out beneath it. The legs belong to Marco, the production assistant.

"I'm trapped," he shouts. "Help me!"

It's heavy, but you lift enough for Marco to slide out. The whole house shakes, and you hear the splintering of wood again.

"We should go," Marco says.

You remember everything falling over outside. You wonder if being in the house would protect you.

To stay in the movie house until the earthquake ends, turn to page 33.

To leave the house and find a safe spot elsewhere, turn to page 36.

Maybe having a roof over your head is best. You follow Esha's lead and head for the house. As you do, a big network of pipes slams to the ground, narrowly missing where you were standing.

"The overhead rain rig," Esha says. "That was lucky!"

You run into the fake house and are surprised no one else is in there. People outside are desperately trying to save their gear. The earthquake keeps rumbling. They don't usually last this long, but today is different.

"This is better," Esha says, pitching forward as the floor buckles beneath her feet.

You're not so sure. People outside are shouting at each other. Then you hear a metallic groan. It sounds like that could be . . .

"The water tank," you whisper.

Turn the page.

You stumble over the quaking floor. You reach a window just in time to see the enormous water tank tip and slam into the ground. An endless amount of water rushes toward the house.

"Esha!" you shout. "We're—"

Your words are cut off as water demolishes the back wall of the fake house. Water blasts through the rooms, washing you toward the front. You slam into Esha, and the two of you are carried to the front picture windows. The windows explode outward in a gush of water.

You and Esha fall hundreds of feet, launched from the movie house. It's a long drop to the bottom of the hill. Neither of you survive.

THE END

To follow another path, turn to page 13.
To learn more about earthquakes,
turn to page 99.

You look out a window. It's too dangerous out there. You look to the side and see one of the production tents is on fire. The disaster movie has turned into an actual disaster—even without any mudslides!

"We should stay in here," you say, looking around. There doesn't seem to be anything else that can tip over on you or Marco. That's a good sign.

Turn the page.

Marco nods and grabs his walkie-talkie. There are voices shouting back and forth to each other. They all sound panicked and angry. They were not expecting an earthquake during their expensive movie shoot!

The house continues to shake, and you get down on your hands and knees.

There's a loud wooden snap, then another. You feel the entire house shift. It knocks Marco off his feet. He lands on his back with a grunt.

You crawl over to see if he's okay. As you do, you notice big cracks forming along the walls. A row of cabinets crashes to the ground, smashing apart.

"We're in trouble," Marco cries.

The entire house groans like it's in pain. After another moment, the ceiling comes down, raining wood and plaster down on you and Marco. The weight of the house collapsing is too much.

You're dug out of the wreckage an hour later. You both survive with broken bones and countless cuts. Lots of bandages means that's a wrap for you.

THE END

To follow another path, turn to page 13.
To learn more about earthquakes,
turn to page 99.

Normal houses aren't always earthquake-proof. Fake movie houses are even less safe. Marco is right, you should go.

"Let's get out of here!" you shout. He nods, takes a step, and nearly falls down.

"My leg," he moans.

"Is it broken?" you ask. Plaster chunks fall from the ceiling, exposing splintered wood.

"No," Marco blurts. "I don't think so."

"Then come on," you cry. You throw an arm around Marco and struggle to help him through the trembling house. The light fixture hanging from the dining room ceiling swings back and forth.

You stagger and nearly fall but pass beneath it. A moment later, it crashes in a heap of metal and glass.

"Close one," Marco whispers, his voice pained.

There are several loud snaps to your right. You turn in time to see the front of the house fold down toward the hill. The floor splits in two, tearing the carpet and sending wood shards up into the room.

The house is going to fall off the hill—and with us in it! your mind screams.

You dig in and drag Marco to the exit. The door swings wildly on its hinges. With a final heave, you stumble and fall out into the bright California sun.

A moment later, there's a groan like a giant dying. You watch the entire house come free from its foundation and tumble down the hill.

After a few minutes, the rumbling stops. You're alive and Marco is too. The crew is shaken, and the set is destroyed. The show must go on, but not today.

THE END

To follow another path, turn to page 13.
To learn more about earthquakes,
turn to page 99.

You don't wait for Esha to decide. The shipping container is close and sturdy. You doubt anything is going to crush it.

"Let's go!" you shout.

Esha is too scared to argue, and she follows you, the two of you falling every few steps. A utility pole snaps and falls off to your right. The transformer slams against the ground and explodes.

The two of you reach the door and crawl in. The container is mostly empty. The gear is all out on set, getting destroyed by Mother Nature.

You're about to close the door when you see others stumbling around. They look like they're unsure what to do.

"Hey!" you shout over the chaos. "Over here!"

They don't seem to hear you, so you whistle long and loud. A handful of people look over toward you. You wave them over.

"In here," you shout. "It's safe!"

You can only hope you're right.

Turn the page.

Eleven more people cram themselves into the shipping container. One of them is Wes Calvin, one of the movie's stars. He's crying.

All of you find a spot against a wall. You all cover your heads with your arms.

The container shakes and rumbles, but you sit tight. Heavy objects slam against it, but you're safe. After a few minutes, the earthquake is over. You survived, and so did the others with you.

THE END

To follow another path, turn to page 13.
To learn more about earthquakes,
turn to page 99.

"Let's get to that house," Esha decides.

The two of you move as fast as you can, stumbling, falling, and dodging hazards.

A car screeches past you, and a moment later, you hear it crash in a crunch of metal and broken glass.

You reach the house and press against the side. Windows shatter above you, and glass shards rain to your feet. You slowly make your way along the wall and knock on the door. No one answers.

Would YOU answer the door during an earthquake? you ask yourself.

You try the knob. It turns, and you push the door open as Esha follows.

"Hello?" you shout.

Turn the page.

“Who’s there?” a raspy voice replies from the dining room. You see an older woman lying on the floor near on overturned chair. Plates and cutlery rattle and fall from the table near her.

“We needed to find some shelter,” you tell her. Seeing the table makes you realize what to do.

You and Esha and the woman crawl underneath the table. You each hold on to a sturdy table leg. After what seems like an eternity, the earthquake is over. You, your costar, and new friend survived.

THE END

To follow another path, turn to page 13.

To learn more about earthquakes,
turn to page 99.

CHAPTER 3

PERILOUS ISLAND PARADISE

Life as a first responder is always unpredictable. As a firefighter working on the big island in Hawaii, you know this firsthand. There are quiet shifts when you and your crew aren't called out for anything. Sometimes, you're stuck at the station, washing trucks, checking air bottles, and doing equipment maintenance. It's hard to believe, but there are days when a firefighter's job is actually boring.

Turn the page.

Today is not one of those days.

It's a sunny day on the island. The sky is blue with a light wind. You felt a small tremor earlier in the day. Living with minor earthquakes is part of daily life.

"Oh, there's one," Kimberly, one of the lieutenants, says while rinsing her coffee mug in the sink.

The tremor lasted maybe five seconds, and then everything was normal again. You are busy checking gear in Engine 1, when a big one strikes.

The quake is enough to knock you off your feet. A sledgehammer from the truck's extendable rack falls, missing you by inches.

The ground is shaking like crazy. Helmets are falling out of the lockers. You and your crew DCHO, which stands for drop, cover, and hold on. You scramble beneath a workbench with a couple others and hold on to a table leg.

You can hear heavy objects hitting the top of the table, but you're shielded.

"We're going to be busy today," your squad partner Makani tells you. "This is a big one."

"I think you're right," you respond.

Turn the page.

The quake stops after about six minutes. It's unlike any you've experienced. You can hear car alarms going off outside. A moment later, the emergency alert sirens sound.

Then the emergency calls start to come in. Help is needed in a partially collapsed apartment building on the other side of town. Another person has requested help after being struck by falling glass. You could go to either place.

To respond to the partially collapsed apartment building across town, go to page 49.

To respond to the patient who was struck by falling glass, turn to page 51.

“I’ll go to the apartment,” you say.

“Nice,” Makani says. “We’re going to need all the help we can get over there.”

You, Makani, Lieutenant Kimberly, and three others hop into turnout gear. You grab your helmet from the ground. Your body still vibrates from the quake as you find a seat.

The truck exits the bay with the lights and siren on. You gasp at the destruction you see out your window. Earthquakes are common in Hawaii, but this one is major.

“Wow,” you gasp.

Some buildings look like they were hit with wrecking balls. Smashed cars are scattered on the destroyed roads. People are out everywhere, faces frowning in disbelief.

“This must be at least a seven on the moment magnitude scale,” Kimberly says from the front of the truck.

Turn the page.

The truck can't go very fast through the damaged roads. Some are completely blocked and impassable. The displaced cars added in make the path to the apartment an obstacle course.

"They're saying several people are trapped inside," Kimberly reports to you and your crew. "Everyone else is out. No fire."

You finally arrive at Sunny Palms Apartments. The buildings are greatly damaged. The top two levels look as though they've crushed the first floor.

To hold back and wait until the building is secure, turn to page 53.

To rush into the building to locate the missing people, turn to page 57.

You're a firefighter as well as an Emergency Medical Technician or EMT. You decide to drive Halia, a paramedic, in the ambulance. You open the bay door and turn on the lights and siren.

As you drive out from Station 1, you gasp. The city is in rough shape. Some of the older buildings are cracked and crumbled. Cars are smashed from falling debris. Broken glass sparkles from everywhere on the street.

"Oh no," Halia says, shaking her head. "This is really bad."

Getting to the scene of the injury is not easy. You carefully weave through the wreckage on the street. There are about fifty others you could help on the way. A parking garage collapses as you pass by. Nothing seems secure.

Turn the page.

You arrive at the scene and radio your arrival to dispatch. You and Halia jump out and find a middle-aged woman bleeding from cuts on her head. A passerby is holding a T-shirt to her worst wound to stop the blood flow.

Halia bandages the woman's head. You help the patient onto the stretcher and load her into the ambulance. It's a short drive to the hospital. When you arrive, you see the hospital looks damaged too.

Patients are usually brought in through the emergency room garage. It's the quickest way to the ER. The patient would receive aid more quickly. But is the structure safe? Maybe bringing the patient in through the front of the hospital would be better.

To pull into the emergency room garage to transport the patient inside, turn to page 59.

To drive to the hospital's front entrance, turn to page 61.

You hop out of the truck as something crumbles behind you. The parking garage across the street collapses. Dust rises from the structure, coating the nearby palm trees in grit.

Makani seems ready to rush in.

"Let's hold back," you say. "Not sure that structure is secure."

"Of course it isn't," he says. "It's already collapsed! Those people can't wait."

"We're no good to anyone if we get killed," you remind him.

Kimberly is talking to another crew onsite. They're putting wooden beams up to support the sagging upper floors.

You can see panicked people watching the building. Some are in tears. You help move them to a safer area in case there are more collapses. Makani sets up a hose line in case a fire breaks out.

Turn the page.

After a while, you and your crew are cleared to enter. You grab a sledgehammer. Always good to bring a tool or two.

You and Makani slowly work your way into the ruined structure. You have to crouch to fit through the narrow gaps where the ceiling has fallen. Only rebar and support posts are keeping it intact.

There is dust everywhere, and you're grateful for your self-contained breathing apparatus (SCBA). It includes a mask and a tank with breathable air. With it, you pull in fresh air and keep your lungs clear. As you step into a ruined hallway, you see a cat cleaning its fur.

To keep searching for the trapped victims, go to page 55.

To grab the cat and bring it to safety, turn to page 64.

You want to save the cat, but you know you need to focus on getting the people out safely. You've read animals have a way of getting themselves out of danger. You hope that's true.

You and Makani move through the partially collapsed hallway, searching each apartment one by one. You find a small family of three and escort them out. You both return to the hall and continue your search.

You come across a doorframe, bent and crooked from the partially collapsed ceiling. The door is stuck, but you pry it open with your Halligan. As you do, you hear the structure creak and crack.

"Hello?" you call into the dusty apartment. "HFD!"

"We're in here!" a younger voice cries further back.

You and Makani work your way to the back room. Things are thrown everywhere.

Turn the page.

You find three teenage boys and their mother. They're huddled around her. She's holding her leg. Makani radios your team's status to Kimberly.

"We need to get you out of here," you say. "This building is unstable."

As if agreeing with you, the building rumbles. Dust and plaster fall from the ceiling. Whatever is holding the second floor up isn't going to last long.

You have two choices. You can try to get everyone out before the building comes down or try to find cover. Makani is looking at the door, then back at you.

To lead the family out of the building before it collapses, turn to page 67.

To find some way to protect yourselves before the ceiling comes down, turn to page 70.

There's no telling how long the people inside have. They could be trapped somewhere. You and Makani jump out of the truck, pull on your helmets, and turn on your SCBAs. The air tanks beep and chirp as the safety devices activate. There's no fire yet, but it's going to be dusty inside.

"Looks like it's masks on," you tell Makani. He gives you the thumbs-up. He's already one step ahead of you.

You grab a Halligan, and Makani pulls a K-Saw from the side compartment. The rest of the crew works to get a hose line charged with water in case of fire.

You don't have time to wait.

Turn the page.

The two of you rush toward the apartment, determined to find the missing occupants. You duck underneath the crushed entryway. You move quickly to a stairwell to find it impassable.

"Blocked," you shout through your mask. "Down the other hall."

The hallway sags as you and Makani check each of the doors. Plaster and dust sift from the ceiling. You hear a distant rumble. You tell yourself it's the truck's pumper pulling water from a hydrant.

As you reach a closed door, you find it locked. You smash the door with your Halligan as the second floor comes down above you. The weight of the concrete and steel crush you and Makani in seconds. You're injured and buried alive. The rescue team doesn't find you in time.

THE END

To follow another path, turn to page 13.
To learn more about earthquakes,
turn to page 99.

The quickest way to the emergency department is through the dedicated garage. You've dropped off patients there thousands of times. The garage entrance looks a little misshapen as you pull up, but the door is up and open.

"We're just pulling in now," Halia tells the patient, trying to keep her calm. "We'll bring you inside, and they'll get you fixed up, good as new."

The woman groans, still in pain from her many cuts.

"It all happened so fast," she says. "Knocked me off-balance, and I fell."

You slowly pull into the garage, listening to the patient recall her accident. "When I got up, the world was still quaking. I heard large cracks and then the glass . . ."

"It's okay," Halia reminds her. "We're here."

Turn the page.

You pull into one of the spots inside. Dust from the ceiling sifts down, coating the windshield. You park the ambulance and hop out to help with the stretcher. As you reach to open the back of the ambulance, you hear a loud series of cracks.

You look up to see the ambulance bay's ceiling coming down on you and the emergency vehicle. The entire garage collapses, crushing you under its weight.

Your fire department is called to the incident. They're able to dig out the ambulance and find Halia and the patient inside, alive. You never had a chance.

THE END

To follow another path, turn to page 13.
To learn more about earthquakes,
turn to page 99.

“I don’t like the look of the hospital,” you tell Halia. “It’s damaged from the earthquake and probably not structurally sound.”

You know big earthquakes can severely damage buildings. There are broken windows, and exterior sections of the building have broken off.

As if to confirm your gut feeling, you see people coming out of the front of the hospital. Patients are being wheeled out in beds and wheelchairs. A man in blue scrubs waves you over and points to the parking lot.

You follow his directions and park away from the hospital. You hop out to help Halia get the stretcher out of the back.

“Bless the two of you,” the patient says, bundled up on the cot.

“And you too, ma’am,” you say, lowering the stretcher’s “landing gear” as gently as possible.

Turn the page.

There's a loud rumble behind you. You watch as the ambulance garage collapses into a pile of rubble. People at the front of the hospital cry out in shock.

The patient is with the ER docs, so you and Halia run to the garage with others from the hospital.

"Was there anyone in the bay?" you ask.

"I don't think so," a woman cries, waving rising dust from her face.

We almost were, you think gravely. You're glad you made the decision not to pull in. It might have saved your lives.

THE END

To follow another path, turn to page 13.
To learn more about earthquakes, turn to page 99.

The cat is in danger. It probably doesn't know well enough to get out of the building. You tap Makani on the shoulder and point.

"Seriously?" he responds.

You nod. "Someone is probably worried sick about it," you say.

"What about the people trapped in here?" Makani asks.

"We'll come back for them," you say.

Firefighters should never work alone, so you both approach the cat. It stops and looks at you. Dust coats the cat's head, its bath unfinished.

The cat meows softly as if asking you a question.

"C'mon," you say. "Let's get you out of here."

You set down the sledgehammer to free up your hands.

"Operations to Team 1," Kimberly radios in from outside. "What's your status?"

As Makani responds, you pick up the cat. There's a slight rumbling nearby. You hear stone and wood cracking.

The cat seems spooked and tries to spring out of your arms. You hold on tight.

Makani looks worried.

"We need to move," he warns.

Turn the page.

Along a nearby wall, huge cracks are forming. You hold on to the cat, and the two of you quickly make your way out. A few moments after you reach daylight, there's a rumble as the ceiling collapses, further burying the first floor.

You saved a cat.

Your crew digs through the rubble to look for survivors. It's difficult, and other workers are brought in to cut through the wreckage. After long hours, the residents are found. None of them have survived.

THE END

To follow another path, turn to page 13.
To learn more about earthquakes,
turn to page 99.

Makani grabs your shoulder. “If we pick up the mom, we can run out of here before it gets ugly.”

You nod. It seems like the best choice. Sticking around and hoping you find something strong enough to protect you seems impossible.

“Okay, ma’am,” you say through your mask. “I’m going to pick you up and—”

“We think her leg is broken,” one of the boys says.

“We’ll be careful,” you promise, crouching down to scoop her up. You’re used to carrying heavy gear and people when necessary.

Makani leads the way through the cluttered apartment. As he approaches the door, the metal frame folds and collapses underneath the second floor’s weight. Your way is cut off.

Turn the page.

"The window!" you shout. Not even two steps later, the entire second floor caves in on the living room. You, Makani, and the family are buried underneath rubble.

You're dazed and hurt but alive. With some difficulty, you reach for your air tank's alarm. You push the button two times. It emits a squeal.

"Team one, status," you hear Kimberly say on Makani's radio. He doesn't respond. That's not good.

The woman you were carrying isn't moving either. You can see her arm through the chunks of rubble and steel. You tap her. She doesn't respond. That's not good either.

A few hours later, you are pulled from the rubble. The three teenage boys are being treated for injuries near the ambulance. Their mother didn't survive, and neither did Makani.

THE END

To follow another path, turn to page 13.
To learn more about earthquakes,
turn to page 99.

You don't think you'll get everyone out before the structure collapses. It's best to take cover and protect yourselves. You hear walls cracking with stress. There's little time left.

You quickly lead the group into the dining room. There's a large table with thick steel legs and a hard wooden top. It will have to do!

The six of you crawl underneath the table as chunks of ceiling begin falling. You and Makani shield the boys and their mother with your bodies for extra protection. A moment later, the upper floor comes crashing down, burying you.

When the dust settles, you see the table has held. You're all safe in a little pocket, surrounded by debris.

Makani calls Kimberly on his radio. "Team one operations," he says. "We've secured the occupants."

You all sit tight, activate the alarm on your SCBA harness, and wait for a rescue team to find you. An hour or so later, you're freed and climb out of the rubble. You help rescuers bring out the boys and their injured mother. She and her family are safe, thanks to your quick thinking.

THE END

To follow another path, turn to page 13.

To learn more about earthquakes, turn to page 99.

CHAPTER 4

DANGER ON THE MOUNTAINTOP

When you think of snowboarding, you imagine big, mountainous regions like Colorado, British Columbia, or the Swiss Alps. So you're surprised to discover some of the best snowboarding is found in Japan.

You and your friend Mei are on your way to a ski resort. You're more than excited. The area has a lot of backcountry areas to explore.

"Whoa," you say, looking out the window. "Look at that powder!"

Turn the page.

Mei laughs and steers the car through the resort village.

"We get over fifty feet of snow each season," she says, sounding like a tour guide.

"Wow, that's a lot," you say, shaking your head.

"Niseko never needs to use snow machines," Mei adds. "It's always the real stuff."

After finding a place to park, checking into the resort, and unpacking your gear, the two of you are ready to go. You're tired from the flight and drive, but the excitement is keeping you going. You can't wait to hit the slopes.

You step out of the lodge and embrace the cold wind in your face. Snowflakes lightly bounce off the goggles on your helmet. The view is amazing. You watch the lifts sending people up to the top of the runs. The skiers and snowboarders look tiny coming down the hill.

"This is fantastic," you tell Mei, your mouth hanging open in awe.

"And we haven't even started yet," Mei reminds you.

You zip up your coat and pick up your board.

"So do you want to do a backcountry run first?" Mei offers. "Or catch some speed on the slopes?"

To head to the backcountry area gates to snowboard around trees, turn to page 76.

To head up the mountain for a downhill run, turn to page 78.

“Let’s check out the backcountry a bit first,” you suggest. “Might be good to see some nature before we shred our way down the big runs.”

“Works for me,” Mei says.

The two of you fasten your helmets and make your way to the ski lift. You clip your front foot into your snowboard and skate your way into line.

When the two of you are up for the next chair, you hop on and pull the restraining bar into place.

“Heeeeeeere we go,” Mei cries.

You’ve been on ski lifts hundreds of times, but there’s still always a little tickle of fear when you get higher up the hill. You hold on to a bar and take in the scenery.

At the top of the hill, the two of you hop off and make your way to the gate. There are postings for hazards and warnings not to go off outside the boundary lines.

You and Mei have skied backcountry runs before. There's always a risk of hitting a tree or getting lost. But you're both seasoned enough to know the dangers.

You both strap into your boards and pass through the gate.

"Try and keep up!" Mei says, heading down the slope ahead of you.

As you shove off, you feel the ground vibrate.

Mei keeps going and then disappears out of sight. Mei is fast on her snowboard, but you didn't think she was *that* fast. You wonder if you should catch up to tell her about the ground shaking. Then again, you could just enjoy the run. You could always tell her later.

To follow Mei by using her trail through the snow, turn to page 84.

To blaze your own trail through the backcountry, turn to page 87.

Starting off with a downhill run seems like the best way to get the weekend started.

"Let's hit a blue square slope," you suggest. "After all this traveling to get here, I need something to wake me up!"

"I was hoping you'd say that," Mei says, play-punching you in the shoulder.

With one foot strapped to the front of your board, you skate off toward the lifts. The weather is nice and sunny, and despite it being chilly, it's brought out the crowd. It's almost a perfect day.

Shredding your way down the mountain won't hurt!

On your way up on the ski lift, you notice the posts supporting the lift cables are vibrating. The chairs swing back and forth. You feel a low rumble.

"What is that?" you ask Mei.

Mei laughs. "Just an earthquake," she says.

JUST an earthquake? you think. "That's bad, right?"

Mei shakes her head. "Not really," she says. "Japan gets around 1,500 earthquakes a year. More than any place on the planet."

"I . . . did not know that," you whisper.

By the time you get to the top, the earthquake has stopped. No one seems bothered by it. You shrug it off. The two of you tear down the hill, and you're in your happy place.

Then the ground starts to shake again even harder. It's giving you a bad feeling. Maybe you should tell Mei you'd like to leave.

To follow Mei's lead and ignore the tremors, turn to page 80.

To suggest leaving the resort until the earthquakes calm down, turn to page 89.

As you stand, trying to decide whether it's safe, the earthquake stops.

"See?" Mei says. "We're good."

You look around. The rest of the skiers and riders seem perfectly fine. It was startling, but no one seems too upset by the brief tremor. There were no earthquakes where you grew up, at least not that you could feel. The worst natural disasters your hometown faces each year are floods.

How can anyone handle the ground shaking multiple times a day? you wonder. *When do you know when a big one is coming?*

"You okay?" Mei asks.

"Yeah, I'm good. Back to the chairlift?" you ask, nodding toward the line of people waiting to get on.

"For sure," Mei says. The two of you skate over to the crowd.

At the front of the line, a chair scoops the two of you up. You're barely a few feet off the ground when the world rumbles again, this time much more severely.

"Seriously?" Mei groans. "Again?"

The pylons supporting the lifts are swaying back and forth. This feels twenty times worse than before.

You look down. It's a short drop, so if you want to bail, you'll have to jump soon. If you stay on, it'll be too high to jump safely.

Or maybe this one will pass too? Mei looks more annoyed than concerned. You need to decide. Now.

To jump from the chairlift while you still have a chance, turn to page 82.

To stay on the chairlift and wait out yet another earthquake, turn to page 92.

This earthquake is no joke. You just know it.

"We need to get off of this chairlift!" you shout to Mei. "Now!"

Mei looks like she's going to say something but nods instead. You lift the bar and bend forward to unbuckle your board. Mei does the same. You watch the boards fall.

"Ready?" you ask. Mei nods again.

You drop from the swinging chairlift, landing hard. The fall wasn't super high, but you still felt it in your legs. Mei hits the ground a second later. You help her up, and the two of you stumble toward your snowboards.

Above you, the chairlifts are swinging wildly. The pylons holding the network of wires aren't going to last long. You made the right choice.

"Those other quakes were foreshocks," Mei says. "Little earthquakes before the big one."

It's nearly impossible to run with the ground trembling. You stumble and pitch forward, landing on the ground again. Your board is right next to you.

You hear people shouting. There's a low rumble further up. A giant wave of snow is coming down the slopes. As if things couldn't get any worse . . . it's an avalanche.

There's not much time before it reaches you.

To jump on your snowboard and try to beat the avalanche to the bottom, turn to page 94.

To move to the side and try to reach an area outside of the avalanche's wake, turn to page 96.

The ground has stopped rumbling, but it has shaken snow from the trees.

What was that? you wonder, unsure.

It's not the best idea to separate yourselves, especially in the backcountry and on a mountain you're not familiar with.

You pull up your neck gaiter and pull down your ski goggles.

You see Mei's track. It weaves though a scattering of thin trees. You follow.

She's really gotten ahead of me, you think, staying on her trail.

And then it hits.

The ground rumbles violently, throwing you off-balance. You wipe out, landing face-first in the snow. You've never been in one, but you know what this is.

"Earthquake," you mutter, through a mouthful of snow.

You unbuckle your boots from the snowboard and struggle to your feet.

You follow Mei's trail until you reach the end of her track. She's disappeared.

The ground stops shaking, but you don't. You frantically look for your friend. Then you realize that she must have sunken into the snow.

You dig where her track ended. The earthquake likely created a pit. You move snow as quickly as you can. Exhausted, you see her bright yellow jacket. And movement.

"I got you," you shout and keep digging. It takes a while, but she's free. You pull her up with your board.

She lies on her back, panting.

"I think I'm done," she gasps. "The mountain tried to swallow me up."

You couldn't agree more.

Turn the page.

The two of you head down the mountain carefully. When you get to the main area, you see the earthquake has damaged the lodge. Some of the chairlift lines have snapped. People are hurt. You can hear ambulance sirens in the distance.

You shudder, thinking of what could've happened to you. You and Mei drive away from the wrecked resort, happy to be alive.

THE END

To follow another path, turn to page 13.
To learn more about earthquakes, turn to page 99.

The rumbling makes it hard to keep your balance. Snow shakes from the trees. As you're about to start off down the mountain, the rumbling stops.

You look around, concerned there might be an avalanche. Glancing up, everything looks fine.

I hope I can find Mei at the bottom, you think.

You carve your way through the snow, dodging small trees. As you pick up speed, the earth shakes beneath your board again. The massive tremor knocks you down.

The rumbling is still shaking the resort. It's strong enough to feel through layers of snow.

Worried, you glance back up the mountain again. Big chunks of snow are tumbling in the distance. Avalanche! The earthquake has loosened a slab of snow.

Turn the page.

You get on your board and race down the mountain. You tuck to make yourself go faster.

The wind whips past you, and you clip a few trees on your way down. It doesn't matter. You need to get off the mountain!

You reach the bottom. Thankfully, the avalanche didn't reach you.

"Mei?" you call out. You don't see her anywhere.

You spend the rest of the day looking for your friend, growing more panicked. She is nowhere to be found.

A rescue team finds her a day later by tracking her phone. Mei wasn't able to outrun the avalanche and didn't make it.

THE END

To follow another path, turn to page 13.
To learn more about earthquakes,
turn to page 99.

You're not used to earthquakes. As you look around, more and more people seem bothered by it. Windows in the lodge break, raining glass to the ground.

"Let's get out of here," you tell Mei. "This is bad."

"We're supposed to stay outdoors during an earthquake," Mei replies. "Too many things inside could fall and injure us."

You see the parking lot.

"Maybe we drive away until things calm down?" you suggest.

"We can't outrun an earthquake," Mei says.

"But let's get away from the mountain in case . . ." you begin, looking up the hill.

Mei doesn't look so sure but notices you're worried. The shaking ground makes it difficult for people to walk. The ski lifts rock back and forth.

Turn the page.

This is bad, you think. You crouch down to free your boots. Your knee vibrates on the snow-packed ground.

"It's worth a try, I guess," Mei says, finding her car keys.

You and Mei stagger toward the parking lot. The tremor has moved cars out of place. A light pole has fallen and smashed across a hood.

You throw your gear into Mei's car trunk and get in. Other people stumble to their cars too.

An avalanche of snow thunders down the slopes. You look away before witnessing anyone engulfed by its icy wake.

Mei pulls out of the parking lot, and suddenly, the car is pitching downward. You, Mei, and the vehicle have dropped into a sinkhole, smashing the front of the car.

You and Mei carefully exit through the passenger door. You climb out of the sinkhole and look down at Mei's damaged car. You're both thankful nothing worse happened. As you glance up at the mountain, you wonder how many people are trapped on it.

THE END

To follow another path, turn to page 13.
To learn more about earthquakes, turn to page 99.

Jumping off a chairlift is dangerous. Besides that, you'll definitely get kicked out of the ski resort. Probably forever. You're also pretty sure Mei wouldn't appreciate you jumping off and leaving her behind.

All of the chairs swing wildly back and forth. People are shouting in terror.

And let's hope this one passes soon, you think.

Now Mei looks worried. She grips the chairlift bar with both of her gloved hands. The chair bucks, like it's trying to throw both of you off. The cables are rolling like big waves each time the pylons shake.

"This might be a foreshock," Mei says, her face nervously looking around.

You know aftershocks are smaller earthquakes that happen days or even years later.

But you've never heard of a foreshock. You're confused.

"Foreshocks are smaller earthquakes that happen before a big one," Mei explains. "Unless—"

"Unless the other ones were foreshocks and this is it," you finish. "The main event!"

As if to show you're right, you see the pylon ahead tip toward the slopes. The metal bends and groans. Everyone screams. People are jumping and falling from way too high.

You cling to the bar, bracing for impact. The cable above snaps before the pylon tips. You and Mei fall to the ground far below. Everything goes black. Forever.

THE END

To follow another path, turn to page 13.
To learn more about earthquakes,
turn to page 99.

You realize the quickest way away from the avalanche is down the hill.

"Let's ride it out!" you shout, deciding for the both of you.

The snow is coming fast, so every moment counts. You plug your boots into the bindings and strap in. Mei does too in a panic. In seconds, the two of you get moving.

The earthquake and the oncoming avalanche keep the ground rumbling. It's hard to stay on your feet. Mei shrieks and wipes out, landing on her back.

"Mei!" you shout. "Come on!"

It's hard to stay up. You look back as the wave of snow buries her and four other skiers. It's closing in on you. You turn to face the bottom of the mountain. It seems out of reach.

Am I even going to be safe down there? you wonder. There's a hollow pit in your stomach. You hope Mei survived being buried beneath a stampede of snow.

The earthquake is still shaking the ground beneath your snowboard. The ski lodge up ahead collapses. People are streaming from the exits, running for cover as glass and wood falls.

As you open your mouth in disbelief, you feel the avalanche overtake you. You tumble and crash in the snow's wake and are buried.

You're battered but alive for a little while. Unfortunately, it doesn't take long before you run out of air.

THE END

To follow another path, turn to page 13.
To learn more about earthquakes,
turn to page 99.

"Let's run to the side," Mei suggests. "Get out of this thing's path!"

She's right. You don't think you could outrun the avalanche. Racing away from natural disasters is something from an action movie, and you're not stunt people.

The two of you move as best you can, but it's difficult. You stumble and fall a few times. You glance uphill. The rush of snow is coming quickly.

Can we make it in time? you wonder.

Mei heads toward some trees, shouting for you to keep going. She is knocked off her feet and falls. You grab her gloved hand and yank her to her feet.

You're in a lightly wooded area off the main run. You're worried you'll be knocked into trees or buried.

"Grab a tree," you shout and find a sturdy one to wrap your arms around. Mei does the same.

A second later, the avalanche hits. The heaviest part of the wave crashes down the slope. A runoff of snow blasts through the woods. You hold on tight, duck your head, and close your eyes.

The snow slams into the trees you and Mei are clinging to. And then, a moment later, it's quiet. You open your eyes. You got out of harm's way, and the trees protected both of you. You're both alive and unharmed.

THE END

To follow another path, turn to page 13.
To learn more about earthquakes,
turn to page 99.

CHAPTER 5

EVERYTHING EARTHQUAKES

Earthquakes are one of the most terrifying and deadly natural disasters on Earth. They can also cause other natural disasters, including large waves called tsunamis, landslides, floods, fires, and avalanches.

Earthquakes happen because of the movement of Earth's crust. The giant slabs that make up Earth's upper layer are called tectonic plates. The plates meet at fractures called faults.

Most earthquakes occur at faults. Heat and energy from deep inside Earth can cause tectonic plates to move, scrape, and bump against each other. Sometimes, they get stuck, and pressure from friction builds.

Eventually, the plates suddenly slip past each other. The energy that has built up is released, causing an earthquake.

Earthquakes are measured with seismometers. These tools measure the changes and movement in the ground caused by earthquakes, volcanic activity, or explosions.

Earthquakes used to rely on the Richter scale that seismologist Charles F. Richter developed in 1935. The moment magnitude scale is used today. It measures the distance a fault moves and the force used to move it. An earthquake from 1–3 is considered light. An earthquake rated 5 is strong and can cause significant damage. Earthquakes that are 6 and above are major and usually devastating.

Earthquakes happen all around the planet every day. Many are so small people don't notice them.

The largest earthquakes occur along the rim of the Pacific Ocean. Eighty-one percent of the planet's biggest tremors happen here. This area is known as the Ring of Fire.

There are four different types of earthquakes: tectonic, volcanic, collapse, and explosion. A tectonic earthquake occurs when the Earth's crust plates rub against each other. A volcanic earthquake happens when volcanic activity changes tectonic plates. A collapse earthquake is caused by small earthquakes in underground caverns. An explosion is caused by the detonation of a nuclear or chemical device.

seismometer

There is no way to prevent a natural earthquake from happening. Seismologists are working on ways to forecast when an earthquake might happen. They study patterns in activity and analyze the data they collect. They also use recorders to monitor tremors. Seeing where earthquakes have happened before helps them figure out where they could happen next. They just never know when.

Earthquakes can last anywhere from a few seconds to a few minutes, depending on the size of the earthquake. Bigger ones last longer. Foreshocks are smaller earthquakes that happen in the same area before a larger one. Aftershocks are smaller earthquakes that can occur in days or years in the same area following a main shock.

Earthquakes may be an amazing event of nature, but they're incredibly dangerous. Having a plan can help keep you safe in these natural disasters.

TRUE EARTHQUAKE SURVIVAL STORIES

In 2023, a massive earthquake shook southern Turkey near the Syrian border. Seventeen-year-old Gülhan Vişne was in her home when it hit. Her building collapsed as she ran for the exit, trapping her underneath debris. Her mother shouted, looking for her. Gülhan used a stone to hit a door to make noise. Her mom finally located her. After being trapped for hours, rescuers were able to get to them. Gülhan and her mom were injured, but they survived.

In 2001, Viral Dalal was sleeping in his bedroom in Bhuj, India. The rest of his family was eating breakfast down the hall. A 7.7-magnitude earthquake shook the city. Their condominium collapsed. Viral was trapped in a small, dark space beneath six stories of wreckage. He was stuck there for five days before rescuers heard his weakened cries. He was the only survivor from his building.

In 1964, Mac Eads and his brother Bob were working along the coast in Lowell Point, Alaska. They heard what sounded like a jet engine, and the ground started shaking violently. A tsunami triggered by the quake rose from the ocean heading their way. To escape, Bob hopped in a car with his brother-in-law, Carl. Mac jumped into a heavy four-wheel-drive pickup truck. The tidal wave smashed into the coast. The truck got stuck on a timber pile. Mac was completely underwater, scared to leave and get hit by the timbers.

Afraid he would soon drown, Mac climbed out. The water pulled Mac toward the ocean. As Mac tumbled toward the beach, he grabbed an alder tree and hung on. The water passed, and he lived. Bob and Carl survived too. The wave had knocked them farther inland. The earthquake is the largest recorded in U.S. history with a magnitude of 9.2.

EARTHQUAKE EMERGENCY SURVIVAL KIT

An earthquake can strike when you least expect it. Having an earthquake survival kit ready to go will save you time and could save your life.

backpack–to hold supplies

bottled water–at least 1 gallon (3.8 liters) per person

non-perishable food

Don't forget a can opener!

flashlight and batteries

first aid kit containing

-bandages

-first aid creams

-alcohol/disinfectant wipes

toilet paper

Bring bags that can be sealed for bathroom waste.

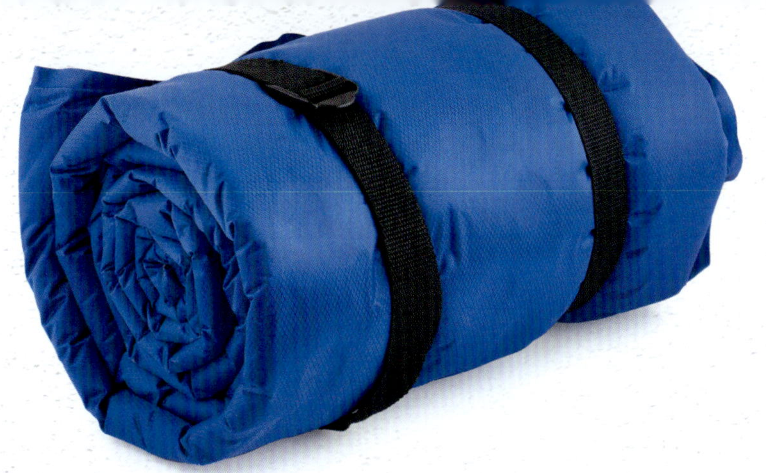

sleeping bag/blankets

multi-tool

wrench and pliers

whistle–to signal for help and rescue

battery-powered or hand-crank radio–for news and instructions during a disaster

dust mask

fire extinguisher

plastic sheeting, scissors, and duct tape–to shelter in place

STAYING SAFE IN AN EARTHQUAKE

Make a plan

Plan where you'll meet up in case of an earthquake ahead of time.

Follow emergency instructions

Use a radio to receive news on where to go if your home is destroyed.

If in a car

Have the driver pull over, stop, and set the parking brake.

If in a bed

Turn face down and cover your head and neck with a pillow.

If outdoors

Stay outdoors and away from buildings.

If inside

Stay, avoid doorways, and do not run outside.

Protect yourself following the Drop, Cover, and Hold On technique.

Drop to the ground on your hands and knees if possible.

Cover your head and neck with your arms.

If there's a sturdy desk or table nearby, crawl underneath it for shelter. If there is nothing nearby to go under, crawl next to an interior wall.

Hold On If you're under a table or desk, hold on to it with one hand and be prepared to move with it if it moves. If you're sitting and aren't able to drop to the floor, bend forward. Then cover your head with your arms and hold on to your neck with your hands.

If trapped under debris, do not:

- Light a match. That could ignite leaking gas.
- Move around or kick up dust
- Shout unless necessary to avoid inhaling dangerous dust

GLOSSARY

aftershock (AF-tur-shok)—a small earthquake that follows a larger one

foreshock (FOR-shok)—a small earthquake that comes before a larger earthquake in the same location

Halligan (HAL-uh-guhn)—a heavy metal tool used by firefighters to pry open doors or break through walls

magnitude (MAG-nuh-tood)—a measure of the amount of energy released by an earthquake

practical effect (PRAK-tuh-kul i-FEKT)—a visual effect used in movies created by using three-dimensional models or figures instead of computer-generated imagery

pylon (PYE-lon)—a large vertical tower supporting power lines or other types of cables

seismologist (size-MOL-uh-jist)—a scientist who studies waves created by earthquakes

seismometer (size-MAH-muh-tur)—an instrument that detects earthquakes and measures their power

turnout gear (TURN-owt GEER)—protective clothing worn by firefighters, also known as "bunker gear"

READ MORE

Brink, Tracy Vonder. *Earthquakes.* New York: Crabtree Publishing, 2023.

Collins, Ailynn. *Can You Survive the Great San Francisco Earthquake?: An Interactive History Adventure.* North Mankato, MN: Capstone, 2022.

Nixon, Madeline. *Earthquakes.* Minnetonka, MN: Kaleidoscope Books, 2024.

INTERNET SITES

Ducksters: Science for Kids: Earthquakes
ducksters.com/science/earthquakes.php

Kiddle: Earthquake Facts for Kids
kids.kiddle.co/Earthquake

National Geographic Kids: Earthquakes
kids.nationalgeographic.com/science/article/earthquake

ABOUT THE AUTHOR

Thomas Kingsley Troupe is the author of over 200 books for young readers. He's written books about everything from werewolves, talking spaceships, and ballerinas to even dirt. That's right, dirt. Thomas wrote his first book when he was in second grade and has been making up stories ever since. When he's not behind the keyboard, he enjoys reading, playing video games, and hunting ghosts with the Twin Cities Paranormal Society. Otherwise, he's probably taking a nap or something. Also, he loves cookies. TKT lives in Woodbury, MN, with his two sons.